Buch 5

SELECTED DRAWINGS
FROM THE COLLECTION OF
HER MAJESTY THE QUEEN
AT WINDSOR CASTLE

HOLBEIN

SIR JOHN GODSALVE (*c.* 1510–1556), Comptroller of the Mint. *c.* 14½ × 11¾ in.

Selected Drawings from Windsor Castle

HOLBEIN

by

K. T. Parker

The Phaidon Press

(CUD)
Oversize
NC
1145
·H66
P3
1954

259.3
H723P

MADE IN GREAT BRITAIN

PRINTED BY HUNT BARNARD AND CO LTD

AT THE SIGN OF THE DOLPHIN · AYLESBURY · BUCKINGHAMSHIRE

PREFACE

U NLIKE his father (a fine artist, to be sure, but essentially provincial), the younger Hans Holbein was nothing if not a cosmopolitan, and in this he showed himself to be a true representative of the Renaissance. Born at Augsburg in 1497, he was still quite a boy when first he changed his domicile and nationality, settling at Basle where he found ready employment both as a designer of book illustrations and as a painter. There were other commissions awaiting him at Lucerne, and he crossed the Alpine passes into Italy, the Land of Promise of every young artist with progressive aims. He travelled also in France, and in 1526 to Antwerp. From there, with letters of introduction from Erasmus to Sir Thomas More, he journeyed further to England, and for the next two years made London his home. On his return to Basle, in spite of every effort to induce him to settle permanently, the first city of his adoption could then no longer offer him the scope that he needed. By 1530 he was back again in England, and there he was to remain until his premature death in 1543, by then to all intents and purposes an English artist.

The Windsor Collection of Holbein's drawings has its equal only in that of the Basle Print Room. If the latter compasses a wider range, not only of time and medium but also of subject matter, the former is incomparable as a self-contained entity in which is reflected the true essence of his genius. For in portraiture, far more than in any other branch of art, lay Holbein's natural bent. A penetrating and highly intelligent observer of his fellow men, he gave us in the Windsor series what amounts to a pictorial epitome of the court of Henry VIII, with all its splendour, its vitality, its turbulence, and its tragedy.

There is something strangely romantic even in the history of the collection. Bound up at an early date in a large folio volume which survived until the eighteenth century, the drawings at the time of his death seem almost certainly to have formed part of Holbein's studio residue. They were probably in Crown possession under Edward VI, and certainly under Charles I. During the interval they passed by gift or purchase through the hands of Henry Fitzalan, Earl of Arundel; his son-in-law, John, Lord Lumley; and afterwards of Henry, Prince of Wales, the elder brother of Charles I. The last named, sometime between 1627 and 1630, exchanged the book with the Earl of Pembroke for the painting by Raphael of St. George, which is now in the National Gallery at Washington. Pembroke's ownership was for a brief space only, and his brother-in-law, the celebrated collector, Thomas Howard, Earl of Arundel, a descendant of the second of the recorded owners, came next in line. At this point information runs short, but so much is certain, that by 1675 the drawings were again in the Crown Collection. There is a passing reference to them in 1690, and it seems probable that in 1698 they narrowly escaped destruction in the fire which devastated the ancient palace of Whitehall. Not till 1727, however, did they properly emerge from obscurity, when, a forgotten treasure, still bound in book form, but soon to be dismembered, they were discovered by Queen Caroline in the drawer of a bookcase in Kensington Palace.

It is natural enough that, after such peregrinations and vicissitudes, a set of drawings executed in a sensitive and vulnerable medium should no longer be in pristine condition throughout. Though the artist's incomparable genius as a portraitist has nowhere been effaced, the chalks - black, red, brown and yellow - which here form the basis of Holbein's technique, have now in some cases become rubbed and tired in appearance. There are also examples where pen-and-ink contours have been added at a later date to imitate those introduced by the artist himself when the salient features of his sitter needed to be reinforced or specially emphasized. The present selection of plates has to some extent been made on the principle of illustrating only such drawings as are still in good, or tolerably good, state. The entire series* including some three or four extraneous items, numbers no less than eighty-five. Among the many outstandingly important possessions of the Royal Library at Windsor, none has so just a claim to be considered a national treasure.

K. T. P.

*A complete edition, with reproductions of each drawing as well as of the relevant comparative material, and with a critical catalogue by the present writer, was published by the Phaidon Press in 1945 and reprinted in the same year. It is important to mention that none of the names occurring on the drawings were inscribed during the artist's lifetime, let alone by his own hand, and that while some of them are trustworthy, others have proved to be incorrect.

Tho: Moor Lᵈ Chancelour

1. SIR THOMAS MORE (1477/78–1535), Lord Chancellor and author of *Utopia*. *c.* 15 × 10 in.

Iudge More Sr Tho: Mores Father.

2. SIR JOHN MORE (1450/53–1530), father of Sir Thomas More. *c.* 14 × 11 in.

3. CECILY HERON (b. 1507), youngest daughter of Sir Thomas More. *c.* 15 × 11 in.

Iohn More S. Thomas Mores Son.

4. JOHN MORE THE YOUNGER (1508 – before 1559), only son of Sir Thomas More. *c.* 15 × 11¼ in.

5. ANNE CRESACRE (b. 1512), wife of John More the Younger. *c.* 14¾ × 10½ in.

6. A WOMAN, UNKNOWN. 14×9¾ in.

Harry Guldeford Knight.

7. SIR HENRY GUILDFORD (1478/89–1532). Master of the King's Horse and Comptroller of the Royal Household.
 c. 15¼ × 11 in.

8. JOHN FISHER (1459/69–1535), Bishop of Rochester. *c.* 15×9¼ in.

Waramus Arch B.ᵉ Cant:

9. WILLIAM WARHAM (1450/56–1532), Archbishop of Canterbury. c. 15¼ × 12¼ in.

The Lady Eliot.

10. MARGARET À BARROW (*c.* 1500–1569), wife of Sir Thomas Elyot. $11 \times 8\frac{1}{4}$ in.

Th:Eliott Knight

11. Sir Thomas Elyot (before 1490–1546), diplomatist and author of *The Governor*. *c.* 11¼ × 8 in.

12. Henry Howard, Earl of Surrey (1516/18–1546/7), military commander and poet.
   c. 10×8 in.

13. MARY HOWARD, DUCHESS OF RICHMOND AND SOMERSET (1519–1557).
    c. $10\frac{1}{2} \times 8$ in.

The Lady Surry.

14. FRANCES DE VEER, COUNTESS OF SURREY (1517–1577). *c.* $12\frac{1}{2} \times 9$ in.

The Lady   Lister.

15. JANE SHIRLEY, wife of Sir Richard Lister. *c.* $11\frac{1}{2} \times 8\frac{1}{4}$ in.

16. (?) ELIZABETH HOWARD, wife of Sir Robert Ratcliffe, afterwards Earl of Sussex. c. $11\frac{3}{4} \times 8$ in.

17. JOAN ASHLEY, wife of Sir Peter Meutas. *c.* 11 × 8¼ in.

18. (?) THOMAS BOLEYN, EARL OF WILTSHIRE (1477–1539). *c.* 16 × 11½ in.

Reskeneer a Cornish

Gent:

19. WILLIAM RESKIMER, Page of the Chamber and Gentleman Usher. c. $11\frac{1}{2} \times 8\frac{1}{2}$ in.

20. THOMAS, LORD VAUX (1510–1556), poet. $11 \times 11\frac{1}{2}$ in.

21. A Gentleman, unknown. $11\frac{3}{4} \times 8\frac{3}{4}$ in.

22. A GENTLEMAN, UNKNOWN. *c.* $10\frac{3}{4} \times 8\frac{1}{4}$ in.

S George of Cornwall

23. SIMON GEORGE OF QUOCOUTE. $11 \times 7\frac{1}{2}$ in.

24. Sir Richard Southwell (1504–1563/64), Member of Parliament and Master of the Ordnance.
    c. $14\frac{1}{2} \times 11\frac{1}{4}$ in.

25. JANE SEYMOUR (1509–1537), third Queen of Henry VIII. *c.* $19\frac{3}{4} \times 11\frac{1}{4}$ in.

26. EDWARD, LORD CLINTON, EARL OF LINCOLN (1512–1584/85),
Lord High Admiral. *c.* $8\frac{3}{4} \times 5\frac{3}{4}$ in.

Tho: Strange Knight.

27. SIR THOMAS STRANGE (1493–1545), High Sheriff of Norfolk. *c.* 9½ × 8½ in.

Phillip Hobbie Knight

28. SIR PHILIP HOBY (1505–1558), diplomatist and Court official. 11¾×9 in.

29. A LADY, UNKNOWN. *c.* 10×6 in.

Edward Stanley Earle of Darbey.

30. EDWARD STANLEY, EARL OF DERBY (1509–1572), Cup-bearer to Queen Anne Boleyn, Knight of the Garter. *c.* $11 \times 7\frac{3}{4}$ in.

Brooke Ld Cobham.

31. GEORGE BROOKE, LORD COBHAM (*c.* 1497–1558), military commander. *c.* 11½ × 8 in.

The Dutchess of Suffolk.

32. (?) Katharine Willoughby de Eresby, Duchess of Suffolk (1518/19–1580).
    c. $11\frac{1}{2} \times 8\frac{1}{2}$ in.

33. WILLIAM PARR, MARQUESS OF NORTHAMPTON (1513–1571), Lord Great Chamberlain.
   c. 12½ × 8½ in.

34. (?) ELIZABETH TUKE (? d. 1554), wife of George, Lord Audley. *c.* 11½ × 8¼ in.

35. A LADY, UNKNOWN. 11 × 7½ in.

Tho: Wiatt Knight.

36. SIR THOMAS WYATT (1503–1542), diplomatist and poet. *c.* 14¾ × 10¾ in.

FitzWilliams Earl of Southampton.

37. WILLIAM FITZWILLIAM, EARL OF SOUTHAMPTON (*c.* 1490–1542), Lord High Admiral.
c. $15\frac{1}{4} \times 10\frac{3}{4}$ in.

38. (?) MARY ZOUCH, maid-of-honour to Queen Jane Seymour. *c.* 11¾ × 8½ in.

The Lady Parker.

39. (?) GRACE NEWPORT (1515 – before 1549), wife of Sir Henry Parker. *c.* $11\frac{1}{2} \times 8\frac{1}{4}$ in.

I Russell Lᵈ Privy Seale.

with one Eye

40. JOHN RUSSELL, EARL OF BEDFORD (*c.* 1485–1554/55), Lord High Admiral and Lord Privy Seal. 13¾ × 11½ in.

LIST OF PLATES

The numbers in brackets are those of the Inventory of the Royal Library.